Messiah

SON RAYS OF HOPE

Poetry By:

Merlin Hellmann

EXPERIENCE HOPE AND INSPIRATION AS YOU READ
THESE HEARTFELT POEMS OF ENCOURAGEMENT

Joshua 24:15 Publishing House

& Lakisha Shaffer Publishing House, Publishing division

www.LakishaShaffer.com

COPYRIGHT 2018 Merlin Hellmann

ALL RIGHTS RESERVED

DEDICATION

I would like to dedicate my poem "Son Rays of Hope" to my beloved Pastor Tim Mullins. He is a Godly and loving shepherd of his flock Mount Hope Community Church.

I thank God for bringing me through a great time of seemingly hopelessness and blessing me with this awesome gift of poetry.

MERLIN HELLMANN

My Sons Poetry

Do you think God for all he's done;
For sending His only begotten son?
Who on Golgotha died on a tree,
To set people like you and me free.

Do you think Him for sunshine and rain?
For giving us a Bible in which it makes it very plain?
That we should love Him with all our heart?
And never from His presence depart.

Do you think Him for your friends,
Who many times a word of encouragement send,
When we're discouraged or a little blue,
Or maybe we have a case of the flu?

Do you think Him for answering your prayers,
And all of your burdens that He shares?
For giving you food and a home?
For giving you a free country in which you can roam?

Do you thank Him for coming into your heart?
And for loving you from the very start?
For all the love God gives to you?
His mercy and His kindness to?

Written by: Timothy Hellmann age 12

DREAMS

A young boy stands there, sad and forlorn.
His shoes are tatter, his clothes are torn.
The code when whips through the young boys clothes.
The boy takes a step forward but that's as far as he goes.

He slowly slumps to the cold ground below.
Tears course down his dirt streaked face as his pain continues to grow.
His stomach is empty, and his heart is void of love.
Rain, cold and steady, begins to fall off from above.

I see the picture so clearly, that young boy in despair.
He lays there alone, because no one seems to care.
He tries to get up but falls back down.
His little heart aching as he survives alone in this little town.

The people of the town past him without a sideward glance.
Some throw him a morsel of food, some laugh at his tattered pants.
He continues to lie there, crying himself to sleep.
He quietly whispers Lord I pray my soul to keep.

But deep inside that little heart lies something that we cannot see.
For inside that heart lies his dreams that will shape his destiny.
He dreams of love and warmth and care.
He dreams of a family, of a home, of a bedside prayer.

He dreams of wealth, and success and fame.
He dreams a dream, he will lay his claim.
He dreams a dream, he prays a prayer.

He hopes for love and an end to the despair.

A young man now stands there with a future and a smile.
He stands at the edge of the same small town to reminisce for awhile.
His tailored suit is pressed and neat.

The towns people once again past him but this time they smile and wave
They don't recognize him now as they gave him the attention he wants did crave.
A tear trickles down his cleanly shaved face.
His wife reaches out knowingly and gives him a loving embrace.

His hopes had given him dreams, his dreams had given him hope.
His dreams had given him a love for life and an ability to cope.
He held unto hope and he held unto love.
He held unto knowing there is a God above.

We travel through life and we travel through time.
We dream our dreams, we live as an integral part of God's great design.
We live through joy, we live through pain.
We live because we dream and see the rainbow after the rain.

If we never forget to hold and never forget to pray,
If we never forget to dream a dream each and every day.
We'll make it through life and we'll change the world.
We'll teach the power of hope and the power of dreams unfurled.

Written by Timothy Hellmann

Forever 17

Somewhere, the sun is shining and little kids are laughing in the park. Somewhere love is born and an eagle floats effortlessly against the backdrop of a summer sky. Somewhere, a mother tucks her children into bed, and somewhere dreams are being lived and hope is being transcribed into reality. But here I lay... lifeless... forever... buried in this cold, dark earth... forever 17.

I was A young man with my future in front of me. I was a young man full of life. I was a young man stepping into adulthood, Full of dreams and full of promise. But instead I lay here never to see the beauty of another sunrise or sunset. ..I lay here... Forever 17.

I had on the money and drugs that I could possibly want. I had designer clothes and the newest sports car. I have all the sex and the women that I could possibly dream of. But somewhere my mother stands over my empty bed. Night after night she slips into my vacant room, and as she stands there she cries an unending flow of tears. She stands there trying so hard to hold onto my memory, yet wanting so much to forget. And as a tear slips ever so quietly down her cheek, she kneels at my bed, and buries her face in my pillow... her heart is breaking. And here I lay, in the confines of an earthly grave. I lay here... Forever 17.

I will never again see the beauty of a fall morning or experience the magic of a summer night. I will never again stand outside on a moonlit evening when the stars are out... and dream. I will never again see a flower in bloom or hear my father call my name. I will never again hug my precious little sister and hear her gentle little laugh. I will never graduate and I will never be married. I will never grow older and realize my dreams. And never again will I feel my little brother tugging on my shirt, or watch him so innocently copy my every move. For I lay here... lifeless... Forever 17.

But I was respected on the streets. You look at me wrong or disrespect me, it was over for you. My boys and I weren't to be messed with, and somehow that made me feel like a man. I was hard, and felt invisible. But somewhere my little son sleeps without a father. I will never teach him to throw a baseball or to be the next Michael Jordan. I would never be able to hold his little hand and have him look at me and say "daddy, I love you. "Because here I lay...forever silenced....Forever 17.

My teenage years was a whirlwind of parties. It was a whirlwind of "fun", sex and selling drugs. I was living it up. I knew everything there was to know, and you couldn't tell me anything. I would never die. And here I lay, a bullet in my head... Forever 17.

I want so badly to smell a woman's perfume, and to fill a spring breeze across my face. I want so much to feel the warmth and comfort of a mothers hug, and to look into my sons eyes. I want so badly to hear music and to feel love, and to wake up in the morning with my little sister bouncing on my bed. But all I will ever know is this dark, cold grave, as I lay here... Forever 17.

Somewhere the sun is shining and Little kids are laughing in the park. Somewhere a father and son walk hand in hand, and life is being lived. Somewhere a young couple walk along the beach and somewhere a dream is born. Somewhere a rainbow stretched stretches across the sky. Above me life goes on. Somewhere... And I lay here... forever 17.

SON RAYS OF HOPE

Merlin Hellmann Poetry

My very first poem

FROM HELL'S DARKEST NIGHT TO HEAVEN'S GOLDEN LIGHT

He also brought me up out of a horrible pit, out of the miry clay, and set my feet upon a rock, and established my steps. Psalms 40:2

Do you tread slowly, life's road here below?
One step more you feel you cannot go.
Sunshine terms to angry clouds of despair.
Life's dark night ---No songbird notes to share.

Midnight pale moon gives light so dim.
Lonely stranger, no one cares for him.
Lilac's fragrant, sweet scent no longer breathe.
Satan wants all mankind to deceive

You're a dear friend also walks this road today. He'll give you strength to take one step more. Rays of sunshine chase the clouds away. Sweet notes of praise slip through midnights door.

The awesome light of the midnight moon glows. Jubilant man, no more a stranger. Dancing raindrops fall gently to the earth below. Thankful for the babe of the manger.

GLAD TIDINGS

For unto you is born this day in the city of David a Savior, which is Christ the lord. Luke 2:11

G   Given to us by our Heavenly Father above.

L   Laid was He in a lowly manger bed of straw.

A   Angels announced His birth-He came because of love.

D   Dashing to the site the shepherds the Savior saw.

T   Tree lights will sparkle and glow in this great land.

I   It is the Christmas Season-Do you the reason know?

D   Down from Heaven above came Jesus at His Father's command.

I   Into this sinful world His love to show.

N   No one who Him sought was turned away from His merciful hand.

G   Gentle and kind is He to all who would Him know.

S   Saving all whom Him seek and giving them a home so grand.

O   Our hope in Him must always be.

U   Under His wings from harm He will keep us free.

R   Raise us up when weary for all to see.

S   Streets with busy shoppers, young and old are they.

A   A mind have they of gifts and celebrations galore.

V   Value of gifts not are they in what you pay.

I   Instead if given from the heart it means more.

O   Only what is given in love is true value I say.

U   Understand do you Christ's gift gave us all an open door?

R   Realizing true happiness and peace in Jesus I may.

W   When will these glad tidings by all be known?

A   As soon as by all Christians the Gospel seeds have been sown.

S   So then the gospel will to all the world be shown.

B   Babe in a manger but now King of Kings is He.

O   Oh, how can one from Him turn away?

R   Redeemer, Friend, and Comforter-All these He wills for thee.

N   Now tomorrow for thee can be a better day.

IS JESUS YOUR REASON FOR THE SEASON?

 Snowflakes dancing upon the busy streets,

Cool breezes whispering secrets among the trees,

Laughing children munching on Holiday treats,

God looks down from HEAVEN and all this sees

All across the land church bells are ringing.

Listen to all those people in those choirs singing.

Hearken to the Pastor as the Christmas message he is bringing.

To Jesus the true meaning of Christmas are you clinging?

Candy canes and gifts piled high under the tree,

Does that more than Jesus' birth mean to thee?

Gifts of Christmas cheer you will give to many far and near.

What gift have you for Jesus , our Savior so very dear?

The Christ-Child in a lowly manger was born.

Years later on a cruel cross His flesh was torn.

That all who will to Him might go.

Repent of their sins and His true peace surely know.

A CANDY MAKER'S CHRISTMAS GIFT

Only a candy maker am I sadly he thought.

No one will listen or by me be taught.

Concerning the love of my Lord so wondrous and true.

How God came into our world as a babe so new.

About the love of Jesus how can I to the children make known.

Smiled then did he. By making candy will they be shown.

Begin will I with pure white for Jesus' virgin birth and life without sin.

Hard and pure it will be. The flavor to many the taste will win.

Into the letter J will I make it so all remember will,

That by the name of Jesus saved from sin we are and our hearts with joy He will fill.

The letter J or the shepherd's staff to aid us in our journey here.

Know may we that Jesus is our Shepherd, Saviour, and Lord ever near.

Ponder awhile upon the awful price of Jesus' sacrifice for you and me.

Include shall I red to tell of the blood He shed to make me free.

Three stripes for His awful beatings to show to us His love.

A big red stripe to denote blood shed from nails and spear on the cross above.

The candy cane thus was made.

Crafted in love it was and from our minds may it never fade.

Remember always how much the love of Jesus did cost.

No need is there for anyone Heaven to miss and be lost.

Written November 16,2005

For God so loved the world that He gave His only begotten Son that

whosoever believeth on Him shall not perish but have everlasting life. John3:16

PEACE IN THE VALLEY

Weary pilgrim, do you a heavy burden carry?

Do you feel you're about to faint under the strain?

Tell all to Blessed Jesus as in prayer you tarry.

He cares so very much and feels your every pain.

Are life's pressures causing your spirit to sink so low?

Feeling hope can no more rise to aid you today.

The fierce storms of your life rage and no peace you know.

As the winds of disappointment your ship doth sway.

In the dark valley so deep there is holy peace.

Given us by our Savior so loving and true.

A Divine peace so pure in our hearts need never cease.

My Jesus gives it to us for me and for you.

Unto the hills look up friend for help is surely there.

From the one who created them and all beside.

On His face you see such compassionate care.

Spirits will lifted be as He with us abides.

So keep peace in your heart as through your valley you go.

Friend keep a smile on your face through tears if you must.

For bright hope and eternal joys are yours you know.

Because in our Lord and Savior we put our trust.

Written 10/25/97

IN TIMES LIKE THESE

If my people, which are called by my name, shall humble themselves and pray, And seek my face , and turn from their wicked ways; then will I hear from heaven, And will forgive their sin, and will heal their land. 2 Chronicles 7:14

Many blessings from God to us have been given.

Countless enemies of our liberty and freedom from us have been driven.

For food and shelter always should we thankful be.

Others far and near have not as you and me.

In times like these people from God have turned.

Our nation so blessed God's love and mercy have spurned.

No kind thoughts of Him as their own pleasures they seek.

Full of sin and shame do they reek.

America our beloved country on your knees fall.

Move back to God and His righteous call.

From all your vain and thoughtless deeds turn aside.

Repent of all your sins and in Jesus abide.

Winds of despair and grief cover our land.

For all that is right in God's sight let us stand.

Back to God hasten we must.

All our evil ways turn from and in Him have complete trust.

Then come what may He will be our guide.

Through each valley will He ever be by our side.

Never leave or forsake us promised has He.

Our hearts full of joy and free will always be.

GOD'S ETERNAL BEAUTY

Beside the sparkling waters gently flowing He leads me.

 The lofty grandeur of majestic mountains do I see.

Sweet notes of praise by God's feathered friends are heard.

All creation manifests the wonders of God's Holy Word.

Sun, moon, and stars by His great hand were made.

Trees stand as sentinels offering their gift of shade.

Busy bees sip sweet nectar from fragrant flowers of earth's array.

Dancing drops of Heaven's moisture cool a hot summer day.

The music of a small child's laughter eases the pain of a lonely heart.

Tears of compassion calm the spirit of one whose companion did depart.

The radiant bloom of young lover's bliss,

Paint a scene we all don't want to miss.

Many are the beauties on earth we behold.

But nothing can compare to the rescue of a soul who to satan was sold.

Avoiding hell's dark terror for one precious soul,

May many more for Jesus we win be our eternal goal.

Earthly gain of fame or fortune will soon pass away.

Everlasting treasures up in Heaven need you to lay.

Pleasing in our Savior's eyes may we always be.

The greatest beauty is a life lived for Jesus for all to see

For God so loved the world, that he gave his only begotten Son, that whosoever believeth in him should not perish, but have everlasting life.

John 3:16

IS THERE DUST ON YOUR BIBLE?

Do you read daily God's Holy Word?

Seek strength and wisdom from above?

God cares about the fall of a tiny bird.

How much more to us He shows His love.

Are you searching for His promises so true?

Learning by the Blessed Book to do what's right.

Giving to Him the praise that is due.

Willing are you to walk in all of His light?

Let not your Bible be covered with dust.

Use it much as your eternal Guide.

All it's words of wisdom learn to trust.

As with our Savior in all things you confide.

Tell the contents of this Beloved Book.

Far and near let others hear,

And then to the Author may they look,

Thus finding for their hearts that needed cheer.

So dear friend, on your Bible let no dust be.

Read it often and pray every day.

Be an example of Christ's love for others to see.

Showing to all you see life's only true way.

MY SAVIOR

Gentle Shepherd, Dearest Friend, I love Thee.

Loving Savior, sinner's friend, you love me.

Eternal love You brought to man here below.

This love You would for us to others show.

Nail-scarred hands filled with compassionate love,

Bleeding Holy feet walking Calvary's lonely road.

His sweet melodious voice calling us to come above,

After we drop at the cross our heavy load.

Loving friend, Oh so kind and very true,

Never failing, always there when needed so.

Giving hope, He will carry you through.

Many blessings on you He will bestow.

From heavy bondage He will set you free.

Put a smile on your face for all to see.

He will give you a song in the night,

As you go on in the power of His might.

A leap in your walk and joy in your talk,

True purpose for life you will with others share

A witness of God's love will show in your daily walk.

Kind eyes of compassion will tell others you care.

LIGHT A CANDLE

In someone's dark corner light a candle today.

A brighter tomorrow will be ours if in God we trust.

Storm clouds of disappointment come not to stay.

Faith that is steadfast and sure is a must.

When you hurt the most, reach out to another,

For in reaching out your own pain seems less.

Always treat others as a sister or brother.

With spoken words always be kind with much fairness.

Give bouquets of praise to the living.

Mankind longs for encouraging words now and then

Lift someone's load by being forgiving.

Better you'll feel if someone's error forgive you can.

Brighten that corner where you be.

Ease a heavy heart with genuine care,

Then more compassion when needed will be given thee.

Help us with each other our burdens to share.

Written December 31, 1998

AMERICA WEEPS GOD CARES

Blessed is the nation whose God is the Lord. Psalm 33:12a

Our America weeps this very day.

Evil forces have shattered many dreams held dear.

For our nation may we all humbly bow and pray.

God still cares and wants toward us to draw near.

The light of hope shines through dark clouds of despair.

No darkness is there so dark that His light can't shine through.

Love, compassion, and unity with each other let us share.

All deeds of love and kindness we can may we do.

Reach out today to someone in need.

Be a friend always for you know not the load they carry.

Behind their smile drops a tear for the life they lead.

Ease their pain with friendship that doth tarry.

Oh America! Fall on your knees!

In the classroom put back God and prayer.

Be thankful for the beauty in the creation of the trees.

Know that no matter what God doth care.

In God's Holy Word we are told,

That if we be humble and pray seeking His face,

Turn from our wicked ways and His hand tightly hold,

Then our land will be healed and our sins He will erase.

Written After 911 September 15,2001

LET US BE FRIENDS

Come my friend and go with me,

As we together travel Life's Highway today.

Many awesome sights we shall see.

Happy together we'll be if we watch the words we say.

Walk slowly we must so we can take time for each other.

We need from each other a kind word and smile,

Let's be friends-All of us with one another.

Gentle and merciful to all as we walk each mile.

Never let us toward anyone hold a grudge,

But forgive others that also we might be forgiven.

If we choose not to than on our life will be a smudge,

And toward pain and despair we'll be driven.

We won't be able to see clearly

God's beautiful flowers and mountains tall.

Because of us not all being friends sincerely.

Help us Lord not between us to build a wall.

Written 03\20\98

JUST PRAISE HIM

Praise Him when sunshine fills your life.

Praise Him when there's darkness and strife.

Praise Him when on the mountaintop you stand.

Praise Him when in the valley you

Land.

Praise Him when great progress you're making.

Praise Him when your heart is surely breaking.

Praise Him when His presence surrounds you.

Praise Him when His promises seem untrue.

Praise Him when peace flows like a river.

Praise Him because He'll leave you never.

Praise Him for blessings large and small.

Praise Him for His love to one and all.

Praising Him makes your burdens lighter.

Also for a future you'll look that's brighter.

Practice praising Him here below.

Then in heaven we'll praise Him forever you know.

When you feel all alone and sad,

Praise Him and you'll feel so glad.

When the road you walk seems so long,

Praise Him and to you He'll give a song.

Put on garments of praise each morning.

Let these be to you, from Him, His

Adorning.

Praising god makes us all very humble.

Help us to praise You Lord and never grumble.

Written 5/16/99

Praise Him and you'll feel so glad.

POEM

And she brought forth her firstborn son, and wrapped him in swaddling clothes, and laid him in a manger: because there was no. Room for them in the inn.

Luke 2:7

Happy birthday Jesus

The trees are arrayed in garments of white.

They stand as sentinels proud day and night.

Thank you Father for your creation so fine.

Truly are you our Father divine.

Stars are twinkling in the sky.

Moon and sun in their own positions lie.

From heaven came Jesus to the earth.

This Christmas season celebrate let us His birth.

Many gifts during this time

Will we give..

God to us gave His precious son

That we might live.

Happy birthday Jesus and thank you for coming for me.

In all things help me. To honor and glorify thee.

As with friends and family you meet this season,

Remember that for this special time Jesus is the reason.

More important to us is He than all the gifts we receive.

The greatest gift was His death that we might believe.

So do not forget to say happy birthday to Jesus our friend.

Tell Father we all thank you that Your Son You did send.

Christmas without Christ is a thought so vain.

Remembering Him will always to us be gain.

Written November 22, 2008

GOD'S BEAM OF HOPE

Dear heart are you weary and full of despair?

Do you struggle each day with many a care?

Your many prayers wonder do you are they heard?

Longing are you for some encouraging word.

Tears flow unbidden down your cheeks.

From life's many pressures you for solace do seek.

Confusion reigns in your mind and heart.

Troubling thoughts seem never from you to depart.

Hearken my friend to a soft gentle voice I hear.

Jesus speaks words that lift and cheer.

Come to me says He to all who are weary.

And I your life will cause to be no longer dreary.

All your many cares I will take.

Carry them on My shoulder for your sake.

Each lonely step will I with you walk.

As together we travel of a future bright will we talk.

Dark days and long nights will soon be past.

Our home eternal will we reach at last.

Worth it all soon we shall see.

When forever with Jesus we shall be.

Written 2/23/04

HOMECOMING

Home at last, oh joyous day!

All tears are past, dark clouds are gone away.

Our victory is complete as we kneel a Jesus feet.

Enemy of our soul is beat as our Savior we meet.

Our children's angelic voices so clear,

Sing praises of our friend who

Gives such cheer.

To our lonely hearts full of despair.

Telling us always he doth care.

Out stretched arms to many friends,

We have missed for so long down here.

Broken hearts then the Savior will mend.

Gone forever will be all our fear.

No more parting from ones so dear.

Eternal fellowship as united we will stand.

Along the river of life so crystal clear.

So jubilant we will be in that happy land.

All trials will seem as naught,

As we gaze upon the one who loves us so.

So glad we will be that the battle we have fought.

As through Christ we defeated our foe.

Written 06/22/97

H IS PRECIOUS BLOOD STILL FLOWS

His royal robe and crown He cast aside.

Love so pure and tender put Him on the cross where He died.

Upon His precious broken body took He all our sin.

So, we could have blessed hope and a new life begin.

Sacred holy blood flowed as angels stood in awe.

Such love as they had never known they saw.

Bruised and beaten was He for you and me.

How can you from Him turn away and not His true love see?

Oh Calvary, lonely Calvary, let me linger near.

Looking into your kind eyes so dear.

How can I do less than give you my best?

Through waters deep must I go but I will stand the test.

It is finished upon the cross cried He.

Despised and rejected was He for thee.

From sin to set us free He the price did pay.

If for Him we live to heaven He will lead us all the way.

Written February 3, 2001

JUST KEEP TRUSTING

Dear saint of God are you tried and. Tested sore?

Feel do you that hardships can you take no more?

Accusations come as a flood to your wearied mind.

No relief in sight do you ever find.

Many darts of grief at you are hurled.

Confusing thoughts all around you are whirled.

Exasperation and desperation in your world do reign.

Pressures and problems enough are yours to cause one to go insane.

Unto the hills do look for God is there,

And in all your distress for you He truly doth care.

In Him just keep trusting He will never fail.

Remember Jonah who God did deliver from the whale.

No battle so fierce or tempest so wild,

Or valley so dark but that He will help His dear child.

Close beside Him He is to leave Him never.

Boundless love to you is given which naught can ever sever.

So, when feeling severely tested and very low,

Just keep trusting for strength from Him you will surely know

Brightness at the end of our journey we will surely see.

When in heaven we arrive with our dear Savior to be.

Written 3/29/04

Let all those that seek thee rejoice and be glad in thee: let such as love thy salvation say continually, The LORD be magnified.

Psalm 40:16

THANK YOU, FATHER,

Thank you, Father, for your whisper of love,

Sent our way through

Evenings' soft breeze.

For the gentle holy spirit like a dove,

Wooing us in all things the master to please.

Thank you, Father, for the peace. You freely give,

Like the calm of the sea after winds bid farewell.

Such joy and happiness is ours when for you we live,

As our grateful hearts with praise and worship swell.

Thank you, Father, for your tender guiding hand,

As You lead us patiently along life's pathway.

We know that all things are subject to Your command,

As we journey towards life's bright eternal day.

Thank you Father for your compassionate tears ,

In the spring's early morning showers.

As your sweet voice stills all our fears,

Wonderful and mighty are all your powers.

Thank you Father for a faith so steadfast and true,

Midst the fierce storms of confusion and despair.

No failures we'll know as we keep our eyes on You.

Deep settled peace we have because You care.

Thank you, Father, so much for giving us Your all,

Through your beloved Son to pay the price for all our sin.

Help us Lord to heed. That pleading call.

To tell the lost how a new life they can begin.

Written September 14, 1997

WE ARE VICTORS

Dear friend of mine, does your path seem dark and long?

Your heart is it heavy with no

Desire to sing a song?

Has satan your whole being filled with morbid thoughts that cause despair?

Longing are you, for someone about you to really care?

Beloved saint of God are you weary with trials and pain?

Does your life lived for God seem all in vain?

Pressures of life, are they more than what with you can cope?

Of a future bright, lost have you all hope?

Forget not dear heart we are not all alone.

For us Jesus died and for our sins did atone.'

Because of our dear Savior's blood we are victorious.

And a home eternal are we promised most glorious.

So bravely march on and stand tall.

In the battle fierce need we never to fall.

Christ is our captain true who will fail us never.

But lead us on to eternal joys forever.

So amidst all your troubles and stress look up.

All suffering will soon be over and with Jesus we will sup.

We victorious through all our lives shall be.

Satan is a defeated for and through Christ we are made free.

Written July 19, 2004

THE WONDER OF IT ALL

Oh the beauty of sunset's evening glow,

As the Master artist paints the final scene of day.

To all the world, earth's beauty He doth show.

Truly He is the truth and life's only way.

Mighty trees of the forest whisper praises to Him.

The brooks and streams make heavenly melodies,

As their waters glide under the moonlight so dim.

All these wonders our heavenly Father surely sees.

Stars up above are winking at galaxies so vast.

Majestic mountains show their splendor to one and all.

Our creator made so much and it will last,

Till we who are ready hear the final call.

All things god made are beautiful

Which no one as a designer can compare.

The greatest wonder is when a shackled soul,

Is set free from satan's evil snares.

Written august 9, 1997

THE BATTLE IS THE LORDS

Stand fast mighty army of God!

The battle is the lords' He has already won.

Each step you take, He before you has trod.

Soon captain Jesus will say come home battles done.

Never weary be in doing well.

Give a loving smile to a lonely heart today.

Of our dear Savior's love to others tell.

May many turn to Him the one and only true way.

When through valleys deep you must go,

Close beside you lead you He will all the way.

Happiness and joy unspeakable upon you He will bestow,

As you march towards heaven's golden day.

Heartaches and tears come not to stay.

Just a few more days and gone forever they will be.

Then all burdens and cares at the feet of Jesus we will lay.

As He welcomes us home for eternity.

Daily thyself deny because you love Him so.

Within your heart hide His precious word.

Such peace divine you will surely know.

Eternal life will be yours.

You can rest assured.

Stay in love with Jesus. He is our dearest friend.

Follow His example with words of kindness as you speak.

The truth of Christ's atoning blood always defend.

Then pray much that others for Him will truly seek.

Written December 24,1999

HOPE

Tattered and torn are the sails of your frail bark.

Fierce the winds of hopeless despair and the long night is dark.

Soon in the sea so deep your grave will surely be.

No future bright can ever you expect to see.

Gone forever all dreams held close to your aching heart.

Friendships so dear have ceased and from you did depart.

Life ahead looks so bleak with one ray of light not in sight.

No one seems to care about you and your awful plight.

Hark my friend, a voice I hear upon the billows so very high.

A voice so majestic and kind is coming and now near you is nigh.

With calm authority speaks He and the billows no more do rise.

Into your vessel the blessed feet step of Jesus all knowing and wise.

Stay on board, safely steer you He will to your home so fair.

Scenes of celestial beauty your eyes will

COME UNTO ME

Sometimes the days seem so dark and long.

Storm clouds all about us truly we do see.

Our spirits sink so low that we have no heart to sing a song.

Then we dear Jesus get our eyes off of thee.

Come unto me says He to us his very own.

Thou art weary I know and to you I'll give sweet rest.

In trials sore that beset never are you alone.

Each day in your life for you I know what is best.

Lean your troubled head upon My loving breast.

Nothing will harm you while hold you I will in sweet embrace.

As a mother bird watches o'er her young in her nest,

So much more our dear heavenly Father cares for us in our place.

The many battles for our souls are very fierce.

No victory without Him can ever we win.

Never a day so dark but that His love will through it pierce.

And lasting peace and joy will reign in our hearts again.

So look up faithful pilgrim, soon all battles will be no more.

Strength for each new conflict Christ will now give you.

Our heavenly abode quickly to we will soar.

If for Jesus a life we lived holy and true.

ETERNAL VICTORY

Weary soldiers of the cross lift your banners high.

For the captain brave and true cometh nigh.

Cause will He the victory to be yours.

If in the battle for truth your will endures.

Satan with many snares will seek to you defeat.

On Jesus always keep your eyes or you'll be beat.

Many evil darts to try your faith at you will be fired.

Remember the battle is the Lord's when you become tired.

No weapon can Satan to harm us use.

When no matter what happens to deny Jesus we refuse.

In every step he our strength will always be.

By His precious hand He'll lead so the path we can clearly see.

Keep marching on for soon will we rest.

Then our hearts with great joy will be blest.

Home at last with angels will we sing.

Praise forever will we give to our dear king.

Written 5/4/04

MYCHURCH YOURCHURCH

Gentle holy spirit as humbly we bow,

Flood our hearts with love that is divine;

No trace of bitter feelings may we know.

As with our friend and master we do dine.

Forgiveness to one and all we do freely give,

As towards heaven's gate we journey on.

For only then we truly begin to live,

Knowing all battles with Christ will be won.

We together must reach the lost.

Encourage each other along the way.

Pay the price, whatever the cost.

Show that God is in all we do and say.

Search my heart oh God I pray.

Let words of thine on my mind to dwell.

Melt me and mold me this very day.

Till I know all in my soul is well.

Fill us each one with thy sweet spirit.

As united for revival we pray.

Help us as a useful vessel to be fit.

That others through Christ find the way.

Written June 6/1997

WHAT WILL IT BE?

No sorrow or heartache ever will abide in heaven above.

Eternal rivers from God's throne will flow of peace and perfect love.

With the angels we'll rejoice and sing praises to our King.

No more evil darts of temptation will satan at us fling.

Trials and testing's will be no more,

For when we leave here we'll go through heaven's door.

Our precious Savior our tears He' ll wipe away in that blessed land,

With his precious nail scarred hand.

Memories of lonely nights will fade away.

Lonely never again will we be on that golden day.

Best of all we' ll be with Jesus and kiss his holy feet.

Patriarchs of old we shall surely meet.

Weary days and sleepless nights we'll know no more,

Once our Savior leads us to heaven's shore.

Blessed sweet rest! Oh how good will it feel!

Heaven soon will be ours' praise God we know heaven is real!

Soon our life on earth will end.

The gospel let us to the world defend,

Sowing the gospel seed wherever we go,

That the way of salvation they will know.

My voice shalt thou hear in the morning, O LORD; in the morning will I direct my prayer unto thee, and will look up. Psalm 5:3

POEM

Whatever therefore got have joined together, let no man put asunder.

Come beloved, let us together walk down Matrimony Lane. Firmly grasp will we our Dear Saviors nail scarred hand. His love upon us will fall as a summers gentle rain. At the sound of His sweet voice will we obey His every command.

Flowers of kindness and compassion will we see each day.
Heavenly melodies from God on songsters will we hear.
All around us the beauty of God's doth lay.
As travel we do upon us will come no fear.

Beside the still waters lead us He will.
And shady green pastures will we be fed.
Joy and peace in our hearts will He fill.
Never leave or for sake us in His word is said.
There will be times when through valleys we will go.
storm clouds will come and dark shadows will appear.
Then words of comfort and cheer up on us will He bestow.
Every step we take besides us will He be near.

Let us prayerfully and carefully walk each day. Keep we must on Jesus always our eyes. Lead us right he will every step of the way. Until one day with Him we rise above the skies.

MY HEARTS CRY

Use me lord today to brighten a weary heart.
Giving hope midst uncertainty and pain so deep.
Look to Jesus-he will never from you depart. He loves you
so much. The price he paid it was not cheap.

The future, my friend, is bright if Him you serve.
Many blessings from his bountiful supply are yours.
So much more he gives us then we surely deserve. Such
joy and deep peace He upon us truly pours.

Abundant life can be yours now and forever. Great help
because our saver gave us his all. Stay, He will, close
beside you, and leave you never. Listen to His voice so
tender and heed his call.

Beside still waters, lead you, He will today. For your
weary body, He will give you blessed rest. Holy garments
of praise on you will He array. In all things for you He
knows for sure what is best.

Let your heart rejoice as we near our heavenly home.
Reunited with our loved ones we've longed to see. Most of
all with Jesus we'll forever there room. Praise God from
all heavy burdens we'll be set free.

MY DESIRE

Oh Jesus, my Dearest Friend, gently lead me. Lead me to some lonely, hungry heart today. Give me words oh God, to help that one find Thee. With love and compassion I'll say Jesus is the way.

Let me shed tears for those who are lost. Live daily in a way that pleases God above all. Help me remember Lord how much your love did it cost. In answer Gladly to obey your Blessed call.

Each day let my kind words always speak,
To those with aching hearts and burdens to bear. Keep May I ace mile filled with love up on me for those who are weak. May all I me know I truly care.

Let the beauty of God's love shine through me. Made my life be a lantern for God in these last days. Shine through me. Made my life be a lantern for God in these last days. Cause my faith to help others see they are need of Thee, and then seek You in Mend in their ways.

Soon Christ will split the eastern sky. We who are ready, what eternal joy will be our own heavens shore. Let us labor for the master, his coming draweth nigh. Will you hear well done as you pass through eternities door?

GOD'S CALL YOUTHS ANSWER

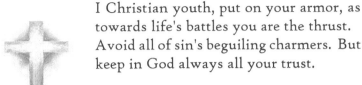

I Christian youth, put on your armor, as towards life's battles you are the thrust. Avoid all of sin's beguiling charmers. But keep in God always all your trust.

Keep to the narrow path every day. Watch and pray as you journey on. Be Christlike in all you do and say. Knowing that through God the battles been won.

Never grow weary in doing well, for a harvest of souls you'll reap, as of the Savior's love you do tell. Of His Live he gave the cost was not cheap.

Dry your tears be love youth. Have hope! God in a mighty way wants to use you. As you with trials and burdens cope, he'll guide you as you make it through.

Keep the bloodstain banner held high, as you lead the church of the future. Don't let the fire of truth ever die. But may you the flame always nurture.

POEM

Let no man despise that a youth: but be thou an example of the believers, in word, in conversation, in charity, in spirit, in faith, in purity. 1Timothy 4:12

Humbly, Lord Jesus before Thee I bow in prayer. Thank-you dear father for your love and care. In paths of righteousness lead me each day. Cause me each moment to know what to do and say.

A life before Thee holy and pure will I live. The beauty of Christ's love, let me to others give. Daily they precious word my constant guide will be. Make me a witness for Jesus strong for all to see.

Fame or worldly fortune, may never be my goal. But rather in this troubled world for Jesus let me win a soul. My treasures laid up in heaven are eternal you know. From God's throne to my heart joy will forever flow.

As a candle burning brightly let my life be on earth here below. Like Christ may I a true example to others show. To do thy perfect will Lord I'll surly try. Please Dear Jesus near me always draw nigh.

*Now faith is the substance of things hoped for, the
evidence of things not seen.*
Hebrews 11:1

POEM

To you God has given another year. May his love for you fill your heart with cheer. As bright as the promises of God is your future here. Keep your eyes on Jesus and close to his side drawn near.

Trials and heartaches move across life's pathway. Much strife from satan endure we surely may. But never will Jesus leave or forsake us in His Holy Word He doth say. On the narrow path that leads to Heaven He'll help us stay.

POEM

Teach me thy way, on the Lord ; I will walk in Thy truth: Unite my heart to fear Thy name. Psalm 86:11

Knowledge and wisdom you've given to me. Forget may I not that it came from Thee. Help me the truth from Thy Holy Word to see. May my life a light of hope to others be.

Every day your strength I surely need. Along this pathway of life please do me lead.
What your sweet voice says I want to always heed. Live I will Lord, as you speak in word and deed.

POEM

What therefore God hath joined together, let no man put asunder. Mark 10:9

Golden sunlight welcomes a brand new day. God's feather songsters make sweet melody. A child's laughter brightens many along life's way. All things bright and beautiful our Father made for us to see.

Upon a voyage so sacred and new will you now embark. Sail each moment with much care and prayer you must. Read daily together God's Word so that your journey be never in the dark. His sweet counsel from the Blessed Book always you can trust.

Sometimes sail you will upon the waters calm and still. And then days will come with boisterous waves and hail.. Safely through it all the Captain will take you- He surely will. From all harm He'll keep you and never fail.

Each day live for God and for each other.
Take time to wipe away a tear and cheer a lonely heart
May the flame of your love burn bright and nothing cause it to smother. The peace and joy that comes from God-
May it never from you depart.

Written For: Timothy and Sarah Hellmann
Lots of love, Dad

POEM

What therefore God hath joined together, let no man put asunder. Mark 10:9

For each other Dear Father we truly give thanks to You. Please guide us safely on this new journey in all we say and do.
Help us each day to seek Your wisdom from above. And never too busy to be a lonely heart to show Your tender love.

Days of golden sunlight with flowers and flower bloom will we see. Also will there be times trials and tests will come for you and me. Let us Dear Jesus under Your wings constantly abide. For promised have You to never leave our side.

I for you and you for me cause each day our love to stronger be. Most of our everyday help us Lord to more e in love Thee. Each day as it comes let us for You and others live.
Quickly when wronged we are will we forget and forgive.

May times of laughter often there be for us to share. Likewise when one of us sheds a tear may the other really care. Until death do us part to each other always we'll be true. In sickness and health may the words be
spoken daily I love you.

LIFE'S JOURNEY

Does the road you travel seem long? With no one to cheer your heavy heart. Crowds of despair and out have you with me no more song? Joy and peace are no more of your life a part.

Our confusion in darkness reigning and your mind? does hopelessness and fears around your every thought? No eternal peace can you ever find. Although with many tears you have sought.

Are you climbing with difficulty a hill in life? And with each step a gasping breath you take. All around you are sadness and strife. You don't know if the hill you'll ever make.

The Master will come walk beside you. He'll speak cheer and warned to your heart. Then bring melody to your so will he and make a life all new. The joy and peace He gives need never from you depart.

His still sweet voice speaks love so pure. With tender hands from despair He'll lift you. Strength through it or He'll give that you might endure. And guidance in what you say and all you do.

Eternal joy and peace are yours for asking. The future can be Heaven for you someday. As in the Blessed Presence of Jesus you are basking..
Praise God you can know you found the way.

LOVE

Father forgive them he did cry,

For what they do they do not know.
On Calvary's cruel cross our Savior did die.
Defeated that day was satan, our vilest foe.

Love flowed in crimson red from His dear side.
A broken heart had a He for you and me.
For all mankind His arms were open wide, Precious Jesus
You gave Your life for all to see.

Awful suffering and shame You did not shun. Meekly
You took it all and never did complain.
The Heavenly Father could not look upon His Beloved Son.
So alone was He in all His pain.

What wondrous love to us showed He.
Taking our place He paid the price in full.
Weary, troubled sinner friend to you call He to come and be set free.
Give to Him all the broken pieces and let Him control.

Peace and abundance will be yours each day. Sweet blessed assurance that happen you'll gain. What close to our Master and heed what He doth say. For soon forever with Him we shall reign.

HEAR HIS VOICE

My dear children, hearken if you will.
To the voice of a friend so sweet and pure.
Your aching heart with joy He will fill.
Give you a true faith that steadfast and sure.

Besides the sparkling clear waters he'll lead thee.
In the hollow of His Mighty hand you are safe from harm.
Goodness and mercy on life's path way you'll see.
Dark shadows or troubled waters are no cause for alarm.

In the valley low or are the Mountain high He'll guide you.
Gentle hands out-stretched beckon to life so new. A life so very free from all dark anxious thoughts. Free as the Eagles flight with prey he's caught.

Eternal joys soon will carry us home.
Free from I heart ache and pain we'll be. Forever we'll all sing, shout, and roam.
Enjoying eternal bliss because of Calvary.

POEM

Our Salvation came in the birth of our Dear Savior. How great was His love to leave all His Heavenly Glory and come to earth to suffer so much pain that we might be saved and obtain eternal life. What an awesome gift was given to this old sinful world who rejected this gift so tragically not knowing or understanding that eternal priceless gifts real value to mankind. How undeserving we were of His Precious love. Wow we were vile and contemptible sinners and hated God He loved us and died for us. Thank God for Calvary and that Precious pure blood that still flows to keep us continuously cleansed. Praise God for the power of the blood which causes us to be victorious through Christ in temptation, trial, or Valley we must needs go through. There is no power that can come against us that is able to separate us from the love of Christ. There is no condemnation or separation. Oh the delight of one's heart to know of a surety that all is well between you and Jesus. The sweet assurance given to us by Jesus brings a calm to our spirit no matter how fierce the winds of tribulations blow. For he is our strength and victory over whatever comes against us. When the enemy comes in like a flood God has promised to raise up a standard against him. We need never to fear but just trust Jesus every step of the way to be faithful as He has promised. All of His promises are sure and will never fail. How glorious to think that our great God, creator of our vast universe cares about and loves us, His dearly beloved children. He always knows what is best for his children and will give to them only that which will honor and glorify His dear Son. May we seek to honor Him in all we say or do.

Oh Jesus our unspeakable gift we cherish Your love and Salvation and desire to give it to others. You are the best gift ever given in for that gift we humbly give our eternal gratitude to You always.

POEM

Put on the whole armor of God, that you may be able to stand against the wiles of the devil. Ephesians 6:11.

From the American heritage college dictionary wiles is defined as disarming or seductive manner. The enemy of our soul is out to disarm us in any way possible he can to lead us away from a true experience with God. He comes as an angel of light at times through people who will speak words that tickle the ears and then stick a dagger of vile and contemptible untruths into our hearts. They should have been on guard against such evil attacks of the devil. For this reason we need to never attempt to live a moment without knowing for sure that the whole armor of God is intact up on our being.

Put on the gospel armor and, watching and to prayer, where duty calls or danger, being never wanting there. Never take your eyes off from our leader Jesus Christ and listen to His implicit instructions with a true heart of complete obedience and unwavering trust. For He is worthy and has never, is now not going to, or never will lose a battle. He'll lead you moment by moment every step of the way in paths of righteousness until one day we'll march into that wonderful eternal city and lay our armor and burdens down at the Master's feet to never carry them again. Look up weary, Beloved soldier of the cross. The Battle will not be much longer. Soon the light of Heaven we shall see and the Victor's crown we shall wear.

O Jesus Dearly Beloved Captain of our souls, let us stand tall, let us march on looking not behind, or to the left or right of us but ever forward to the eternal goal set before us.

Look Up

Do the angry clouds of your life,
Shed bitter tears of anxiety on your very soul?
All around you rains confusion and strife.
Your mind is so weary as dark thoughts take their toll.

Your ship on life see Carrie sells tattered and torn.
No lighthouse do you see through the dark night.
Your heart grows heavy and so very forlorn
Darkness and distraction Shirley are your plight.

Look up weary check out, tis a voice so sweet I here
Calling through the storm clouds of life.
Speaking to your heart such peace and cheer,
Soon you'll be home and no no more strife.

The blessed Lord who allows in our lives stormy trials,
Also brings golden sunlight and refreshing rain.
Be faithful and someday Jesus will give a smile.
As he welcomes us home to his eternal reign.

So when you feel no more you can take,
Look up to Jesus for added strength and grace.
Help you He will heavens shore to make.
And they are you will look into His blessed face.

One day all life's battles will seem as naught.
All sickness and pain will dash away.
When Jesus returns and in the clouds we're caught.
As we enter heavens glorious eternal day.
Written 2/08/98

Heaven! Don't You Want to Go There?

I'm heading for the blessed promised land.
No tears were dim the eyes on Heaven's shore.
My every step is at His full command.
He knows best My Savior the One I adore.

He's promised to never leave or for sake me.
Through each Valley close beside me He walks.
So glad I am I from bondage to be set free.
His sweet voice to me bring such comfort as He talks.

Soon I'll see the One who gave His all.
Then that Blessed hope will be mine.
What joyous day when I hear that final call.
Then as the stars I'll forever shine.

Heartaches will be remembered no more.
Flowing eternally as a rushing river will be peace.
Storm clouds of life will make their exit through God's door.
Trials and pain in our lives will cease.

Oh, my friend won't you to have heaven go?
Make a right between God and you.
Get rid of our anger and strife here below.
Go God's way and a life you'll enjoy that is new.

Don't wait to make your peace with God. No matter what you've done He for you doth care.
Never on the Savior's precious blood trod.
Heaven is real! Don't you want to

POEM

And Samuel said, Hath the Lord as great delight in burnt offerings and sacrifices, as in obeying the voice of the Lord? Behold to obey is better than sacrifice, and to hearken than the fat of rams. 1 Samuel 15:22

No matter how many patterns your mode of life portray to the outside world of your living for Jesus in word and deed, if you are not in complete obedience to His will for your life from your heart, all is in vain. Therefore you will not be presentable to Him on that glorious day of His appearing to take us home who love Him with our whole heart. In every avenue of our lives it is not what we will but rather what He wills in all our thoughts, words, and deeds that the glory would always be His in Spirit and Truth. Our obedience to Him is not because of fear but because we love Him and delight to do His will and that causes Him to the light in us as His obedience and loving children. He's done so much for us and giving us the best He has in His precious Son Jesus and so therefore we need to out of a grateful and loving hearts give Him all of our thanksgiving, praise and love which is due Him. He is so worthy and we are so neglecting in giving Him His rightful Praise and Honor. Praise be to the Father! Praise be to the Son! Praise be to the Holy Ghost!

Father Dear, Abba Father Grant to us hearts full of deep thankfulness and ardent Praise for who you are and all the blessings you continuously pour on us even though we fail you so often and many times are sold slow to see our failures and repent of them. You Lord are our whole life and all we ever hope and trust to be.

POEM

Thy rod and thy staff they comfort me. Psalms 23:4.

Even gods rod of correction is a comfort because He corrects us because He really cares about us and loves us dearly. Help me Lord to go through cheerfully are you lead me through, that I might glorify and honor you. You will not lead me through any valley that you won't walk close beside me in. Jesus went through suffering because of love knowing that His love would be rejected and His precious blood trampled. What a awesome Savior and friend! I love Him so. He loves me too.

I have nothing to give but myself completely, and to love Him with all my heart. To put a smile on the Blessed face of Jesus is worth more than all the riches of the world combined. Just to know that I'm pleasing Him in all I say or do makes me full of unspeakable joy.

Thank You

Son Rays of Hope

PRAYER OF SALVATION

If you have not accepted the Lord Jesus as your Lord and Savior and want to be saved. Say this prayer: My father in heaven, I am a sinner in need of a Savior, Jesus I believe in you that you're the Christ and that God raised him from the dead. Please come into my heart and become my Lord and Savior. If you just pray that prayer and have made Jesus the Lord over you and your life, you are now part of God's family!

The Bible teaches: But what does it say? "The word is near you, in your mouth and in your heart" (that is, the word of faith which we preach): that if you confess with your mouth the Lord Jesus and believe in your heart that God has raised him from the dead, you will be saved For with the heart one believes unto righteousness, and with the mouth confession is made unto salvation. For the Scripture says, "Whoever believes in him will not be put to shame." Romans 10:8–11, NKJV

Made in the USA
Columbia, SC
08 June 2020